How To Find The Right Man and

Become His

Center of Attention

Anyone can find a man. . . Let me

show you how to keep him.

Debra Clifton Mitchell

Dedication

I would like to dedicate this book to my three favorite people in this world. They are affectionately known as my "Dream Team".

Dwayne Sr. – the love of my life and best friend.

Danielle – our daughter and world traveler.

Dwayne II – our son and Eco-Ambassador.

I love you.

Debra Mitchell

Special Thanks to:

- *Marleena Mitchell*

  Cover Design and Artwork

- *Danielle Mitchell*

  Editor in Chief

Table of Contents

One

Dreams Do Come True

I met my husband thirty-one years ago. We have been married for twenty-three years. I can honestly say, I found my soul mate, and we are very happily married. After all of these years, I'm still very excited to be Mrs. Dwayne Mitchell.

Like most little girls, I dreamed of getting married and living happily ever after. However, with the divorce rate between 50 – 60%, it is becoming more and more difficult to realize this dream. A traditional family with a husband and wife with their natural children is now the exception instead of the rule. A large percentage of married couples constantly fight against each other instead of working together creating an unhealthy environment for all involved. As a result, numerous homes across this country are headed by single or divorced women.

I've often thought we are asking couples to do something nearly impossible. Having a long term, loving relationship with their soul mate is attainable. How can they do this if they have never seen a healthy, solid marriage with two people who love and support each other? What can they use as a pattern for their marriage? If all they have seen is confusion, fighting, and drama, what would encourage them to marry? And if they do decide to marry, what would make them stay in a marriage for the long haul?

I have mentored many young women over the years. However, I never thought I spent enough time trying to teach them how to find a great relationship, keep it alive, and beat the odds. This is what I am going to do now.

My hope is that the women who read this book will get the tools needed to become their man's center of attention. Why not learn from my experiences, try to avoid some common mistakes and get it right the first time? These are the comments that I heard over and over again and inspired me to write this book.

When I was a young girl looking for advice, I got none. I learned by trial and error. What a haphazard way to make one of the most important decisions of your life: choosing your husband – the man you want to spend the rest of your life with.

Two

Are you ready to be in a relationship?

Just because he's handsome and you are free that evening, doesn't mean you are ready to be in a relationship. When I met my husband, I was a college freshman. I knew I was not ready or interested in being in a serious relationship. The deciding factor for me was the time commitment that I invested in the relationship. At age 18, I wanted to concentrate on my studies, join a sorority and hang out with my friends.

I've observed one fatal mistake made by women of all ages. They make themselves readily available from day one. Now the man thinks she is boring. They never experienced the excitement of a new relationship. I agree that physical attraction and chemistry is very important, but we must look deeper than that.

How can you express interest in a man and still allow him to pursue you? There is a way to do this without chasing or stalking him. After all, don't you want to know how he really feels about you? If he pursues you, it confirms that he is interested in you.

I suggest you exchange numbers and then wait a week for him to contact you. Don't get me wrong, I don't think you should play games with people. Instead, what I am suggesting is that you continue to do the things that are important and of interest to you. I'm sure you have plenty of other things you need to do with your valuable time. After a week, give him a quick call and tell him you enjoyed meeting him last week and would like to hang out sometime. If he hesitates or doesn't respond favorably, you know that he is not the one. I know what you are thinking. How can he not be interested in this beautiful and intelligent woman standing right in front of him? It happens every day. Aren't you glad that you didn't put all of your time and energy into him?

I've heard so many women across cultures, income brackets, and age brackets admit that they gave up everything they valued for a man. And with the divorce rate so high, what do they have when he's gone? – Nothing! The truth is they probably were not ready to be in a relationship in the first place. Take time, a great deal of time to know and love yourself. You should never feel like a fish out of water in your own relationship or marriage.

One thing I admire about my husband is his self confidence in all situations. He is very proud to be the head of our household. We complement each other without competing against each other. When we were dating, he did not try to control our time together. When we were free, we hung out together. There are times when he was busy with his interests and so was I. I didn't feel pressured to be with him.

Ladies, we are whole with or without a man. A man cannot complete you. When you and your potential man both know this, you just might be ready to be in a relationship – and become his center of attention.

Three

Looking For Love

Where are you looking for your soul mate? Is it the club or local bar? If so, you are wasting your valuable time. The men who frequent those establishments are looking for a quick, cheap thrill. Is that what you consider yourself?

Also, never date a married man. This is a total waste of time. I can't count the number of women who have wasted valuable time waiting for a married man to leave his wife. This day rarely comes. And if it does and he marries you, there's a great chance that he will cheat on you too. Past behavior is a great indicator of future behavior. Can you really trust a man like this? What kind of marriage can you have without trust? This same rule applies when it is common knowledge that he is in a relationship – especially if he lives with his girlfriend.

I realize a married man is not going to come right out and tell you that he is married. Therefore, you have to look for the tell-tale signs. Here are a few for starters.

Does he only give you a cell phone number? Does he tell you what time of the day or night to call? Why can't you call when you want to? What is his home address? Why doesn't he invite you over? Is he unavailable during the holidays or his birthday? Why can't you meet his family? Everybody is related to somebody. If he tells you his whole family is deceased, he is lying. You are looking for your prince, not one to share with the whole neighborhood.

Why not raise your standards and try something that could lead to that long term relationship? I believe everyone has their own set of skills, talents, and abilities. What are you doing with yours? Live <u>your</u> life. Are you with a partner that embraces your unique greatness or does he try to stifle it? Does he feel threatened by it?

If you are a high school or college student, what activities or clubs can you join with people of similar interest? For example, do you want to become an entrepreneur some day? Why not form an Entrepreneur's Club at your school? It's a great place to meet people who can share ideas. You never know, your soul mate and future business partner might be there.

If you are out of school, what are you interested in? Do you have any hobbies? What are you passionate about? How do you spend your free time?

Do you love to travel? Do you like working in your yard planting trees and flowers? There is something you do that comes naturally to you. Find people of similar interest to spend your time with.

Do you like political, social or community activities? Great! You can meet all kinds of people in these groups. Maybe consider running for office as the Village Clerk or run for President of the Chamber of Commerce. If you have children, you can become involved in the Parent Teachers' Association. There are numerous single parents raising their children these days.

Are you the athletic type? Why not participate in your sport on a regular basis? For example, join a bowling league or play volleyball or basketball once a week. Women are just as competitive in sports as men.

It is very common to see married couples in the same profession. I know plenty of couples where both are politicians, physicians, business owners, educators, lawyers, athletes, etc. My husband and I both have Masters' Degrees in our respective fields. He has a Master of Health Science in Health Services Administration. I have a Master of Business Administration.

Couples who have several common interests can always find something to talk about. Constant communication is key in any relationship, especially a marriage.

Four

Identifying Abusive Relationships

Now you've found a great guy with interest common to yours. Let's talk about some common mistakes that I've seen many times over the past thirty years.

I can't even count how many women who find a man with fatal flaws and somehow think they can change him. Let me clear this up now, it cannot be done! The only person you can change is yourself.

I grew up with an uncle and cousin who were both alcoholics. I've seen firsthand the impact alcoholism has on the family. Both died young – ages 42 and 50 respectively. They were verbally, physically, and psychologically abusive to their wives and children. As a result, I decided as a teenager that I would not date a man who drank alcohol or did any type of drugs. I understood back then that I could not change another person.

Let me explain something that really concerns me. Some women enter and remain in abusive relationships. Abuse comes in several forms. There are men who will convince you that as long as you don't need medical attention, you have not been abused. This could <u>NOT</u> be further from the truth.

Unfortunately, I know women who fit in all categories of abuse. Here are some brief definitions of the major forms of abuse.

Emotional/Psychological Abuse

Emotional and or psychological abuse is designed to control or defeat another human being. It can come in the form of fear, humiliation, intimidation, guilt, coercion, and manipulation. It wears away at your self confidence and self worth.

As a result of emotional abuse, a person feels useless, never good enough, never pretty enough, etc. I have seen beautiful and intelligent women who are in this type of relationship. However, they think they are ugly and stupid.

Verbal Abuse

Verbal abuse involves the use of language. It is a form of profanity and includes words that are insulting, disrespectful, rude, vulgar, critical, and sarcastic. Often this abuser goes "verbally ballistic" without cause. It has the same purpose as emotional abuse - to tear down your self esteem and self worth. Does he have a problem with gambling, alcohol, or drugs? Many of these men are emotionally and verbally abusive.

Economic or Financial Abuse

Economic or financial abuse occurs when the man is not supporting his family. The man is the head of the household and when he takes a wife, he has the responsibility for providing for her and the children.

This is a form of domestic abuse in which the abuser uses money or lack thereof as a means of controlling his partner. They do not allow their partner to see bank records, bills, or credit cards. Some refuse to work to make enough money to cover the household bills. Therefore, putting the burden upon their partners to keep the household running. Some abusers demand an account for all money spent even for personal items, such as deodorant and feminine products.

Physical Abuse

Physical abuse is intended to cause feelings of intimidation, pain, injury, and harm. It can also lead to death or permanent disability. Physical abuse includes striking, punching, slapping, kicking, whipping, beating, strangling, head butting, sleep deprivation, exposure to cold or heat, burning, and biting.

Sexual Abuse

Sexual abuse is sexual activity without the consent of the victim, often with the threat of violence. If you are required to participate in unwanted, unsafe, or degrading sexual activity – this is a form of sexual abuse. It can also include date rape and unwanted sexual contact between married couples. Men have been charged and convicted of raping their wives in the past. No means no, even between married couples.

If your man is abusive before the wedding – guess what? He's going to be abusive after the wedding. A wedding ceremony lasting 15 minutes will not change a man. I've attended countless weddings and listened to brides brag about how they are going to change their men right after the wedding.

You are living in denial if you think you can change him. I have interviewed hundreds of women who realize that after 15-20 years that their man is not going to change. However, at this point, they have children together.

If you are raising children in an abusive home, how do you think it is affecting them? Many children with behavior/emotional problems often come from abusive homes. By continuing to stay in abusive homes, you are continuing a vicious cycle. I'm sure this is a contributing factor to the rising divorce rate in this country.

So my advice is to avoid the pitfalls and get out of the relationship early. Ask yourself this critical question. "Do I want to live the rest of my life this way?" I'm sure I know the answer. It is without hesitation "no".

If your man is serious about healing himself, he will get counseling and stay there on his own. It's not to win you back, but to become better able to deal with his issues. You can't love him enough to cure him. He needs professional help, and he has to want it and be willing to stick with it. Love feels good. It doesn't hurt emotionally, verbally, economically, physically, or sexually.

Ladies, he is not your boo, he is your boo-boo! Cut your losses. Get out and stay out!

Five

Intimacy

You and your man have been getting along beautifully and you are thinking about becoming intimate with him. I am against sexual activity early in the relationship for all of the obvious reasons. I honestly think you need to determine if he is worthy of sharing something so special. This is why waiting is a good thing!

I'm sure every woman has a set period of time in mind before considering intimacy. However, I want you to think about a few more things before you find yourself naked.

You don't know how many partners he's had. You probably don't know anything about his sexual health. How can you protect yourself? You must to be your own health advocate. Carry condoms in your purse if you are even thinking about sexual intercourse. Also, you should visit your gynecologist to determine the best birth control method for you.

If you are going to be sexually active, you must become responsible. Always, always, practice safe sex. If he refuses to wear a condom, then there will be no sexual contact of any type. It is possible to contract diseases orally as well as vaginally. Your gynecologist will give you all of the information you need on sexual transmitted diseases, HIV, and AIDS.

Don't be fooled into thinking it can't happen to you. It can and will if you don't protect yourself. Just to make myself clear, you must use birth control to prevent unwanted pregnancies. He must wear a condom to prevent sexually transmitted diseases <u>every</u> time you have intercourse

I've heard couples say that when you have to plan time for intimacy, it takes away the excitement. I beg to differ. Why not let your man anticipate what an intimate encounter with you will be like? You can plan a romantic interlude with him.

One thing my husband and I have done over the years is plan several weekend get-a-ways. Just he and I – no children and no cell phones. We usually travel about three hours away so we can talk to each other along the way. I flirt with him all the way. He has the sexiest eyes and devilish grin that still makes my heart race. It is a great way to reconnect.

There's always excitement in a hotel room because you are in a different environment. Bring his favorite lingerie and a CD with his favorite love songs. Have champagne delivered to the room. Give him a night to remember. Treat this time together as a mini-honeymoon.

When he's asking when the two of you can go away together again – you know you've become his center of attention.

Six

Get Prepared To Do Your Homework

Women can talk for hours about men. A common topic of discussion is "How long should a couple date before getting married?" Of course, there is no magical period of time. Instead, let's take a realistic approach to one of the most important decisions you will make in your life. You must do your homework before agreeing to enter in a marriage.

Everyone knows your man is going to be on his best behavior early in the relationship. I think you should wait at least a year to allow yourself time to really get to know him. You need to observe him through all of the major events during the year.

How does he celebrate the holidays? Are they a big deal for him or just another day? Does he participate in family reunions? Is he happy to introduce you to his extended family? What does he do for you on your birthday? If you already have children, does he acknowledge you on Mother's Day?

Is he active in his place of worship? Is this important to you? What faith do you want to introduce to your future children? Is it the same as your potential husband's? Is this important to you? What are his views on raising children? What does he think is appropriate discipline for children? Do you agree or disagree? Carefully observe him in his apartment or home. Is it neat and orderly or is it in disarray? Which is acceptable to you?

Now it's time to look for some subtle signs of abuse. Let's start with economical or financial abuse because it is easy to detect. Does he have a steady and verifiable source of income? Is it enough to cover all of his monthly bills? Does he make excuses for not working full time? Does he say he's "not the type" to work a typical job? Is he a grown man living at home with his mother? Why doesn't he have a place of his own? Does he have his own car or is he driving his mother's?

Does he pay his own bills on time or do you see late notices every time you go by his place? Do you see a stack of bills that have not even been opened? Do you fight with him about paying bills? How do you expect him to support you and your future children if he can't even pay his own personal expenses? Does he have children from a previous relationship? If so, is he paying child support on a monthly basis? If not, why have a child with him? Your baby will be another child in the world not being supported by both parents.

Don't make excuses for him. It is – what it is. Do you want to live the rest of your life this way?

Here are a few signs of emotional abuse. Does he try to keep you from your family and friends? Does he constantly keep tabs on you? Does he limit your ability to use the phone, car, or money? Does he act excessively jealous and possessive? Does he destroy furniture or abuse the pets?

How are you starting to feel about yourself? Do you doubt your own judgment? Are you depressed all the time? Do you doubt your memory of events after an outburst? Does he have a problem with gambling, alcohol, or drugs and blame it on you? Are you now afraid of him? It's time for that critical question. Do you want to live the rest of your life this way?

Unfortunately, verbal abuse is very common. Does he constantly call you vulgar names? Does he criticize or humiliate you even in front of your family, friends and children? Does he threaten you? Does he intimidate you? Does he constantly disrespect you and tell you that you can't do anything right?

Are you walking around on egg shells just to avoid another violent outburst? You know the drill. Do you want to live the rest of your life this way?

Sexual abuse is often harder to detect. If you are not interested in sexual activity, can you say no without causing a fight? After all, you are in control of your own body. Does he pressure you to have more children when you don't want anymore? Do you feel violated in your own bed? If so, these are signs that you could have been a victim of sexual abuse. It's time to revisit that critical question again. Do you want to live the rest of your life this way?

Physical abuse is very serious. Many women die at the hands of their abusers. You hear stories about this nearly every day. Check the statistics – they are staggering. It is the most unreported crime in America. Seriously, do you want to live the rest of your life this way? How you answer can be the difference between life and death. Please be honest with yourself and choose wisely.

I know this seems like a lot of homework, but don't you think you owe it to yourself to really get to know the man you are contemplating marriage? Over the years, I've observed many women who spend more time researching a new car than they do researching their husbands.

Those whirlwind courtships lasting a few weeks or months more often than not, end in divorce.

Once the wedding is over and you settle into everyday life, this is the person you've agreed to spend your life with. You need to thoroughly understand what you are working with. This is of course a short list of abusive behavior. It is intended to be food for thought.

Seven

A Child Will Not Make A Marriage Last

Should you marry a man just because you are pregnant or have a child together? I have been asked that question by women of all ages and backgrounds. My answer is no. I base my answer on my observations of couples over the past 30 years. Most of them have broken up because they were never meant to be. Those few that stay are miserable and as soon as the child leaves home, they are gone.

Remove the child from the equation and ask yourself if you still want to spend time with this person. What do you have in common? Do you have similar interests or hobbies?

When you are together, is there peace and harmony or are you always fighting? What does your family think of him? Do they call him a "loser" because of the way he treats you or make you feel? Our families know us better than we realize. They can tell when we are upset or trying to make excuses for him. If you can't be yourself, this is a sign you need to get out of this relationship.

If you have a child together, you should concentrate on being co-parents – not lovers or man and wife. It is better for a child to grow up in two separate loving homes, than one dysfunctional home. Also, why waste time with Mr. Wrong? This is valuable time you should be spending with your soul mate - the one who only has eyes for you.

Eight

Fighting Fair

Unfortunately, we kiss a few frogs before finding our handsome prince. So you've met this great guy and have many common interests. There is no evidence of any form of abuse or addiction.

How do you handle spats, conflicts, and or disagreements with your man? It is going to happen sooner or later. Ladies, we can't expect our man to treat us with love and respect, and we are abusive to him. Women can be abusers too. Learn how to fight fair.

The number one rule – do not talk about his mother or father. Parents are off limits. If the problem involves one of them, figure out <u>together</u>

some ways to handle the situation so it doesn't occur again.

Next, do not point out your husband's flaws in the middle of an argument. This is not the time or place. I'm sure you don't want your flaws highlighted. Avoid adding more drama to the situation. Stay focused on the problem at hand.

Finally, don't argue about irrelevant and minor things. So what if he doesn't put the cap on the toothpaste or put the wrong item in the recycle bin. He probably doesn't like the way you do some things, but he overlooks them. Why can't you? Remember, you are not perfect either.

I also suggest a cooling off period. You don't want to say or do something stupid. I've learned the hard way that is it not good for me to talk about things when I am very upset. Clear your head before trying to talk to your mate.

I often write down what is bothering me before I talk it over with my husband. Then I wait a couple of days so I can talk to him calmly. You have to learn to speak up for yourself. If something has occurred that is unacceptable to you, now is the time to address it.

Nine

Mother-In-Laws

Now it's time to size up the competition. I don't mean the other ladies who think your man is handsome - I mean his mother. Mother-in-laws have been ruining marriages for many years. Don't let her ruin yours.

It's normal and natural for a mother to love her son and want the best for him. However, now since you have come around, she may feel threatened because you are becoming his center of attention. This may be more apparent if his mother is single, divorced, or widowed and doesn't have a man of her own.

I'm sure you've seen cases where grown men are considered "mamma's boy", simply because they can't make a move without consulting their mother.

First things first – What kind of relationship does he have with his mother? Does he acknowledge her on her birthday or Mother's Day? I think this is great. As a wife and mother myself, I expect to be acknowledged on important dates. However, if she thinks she has a vote in how you handle your business, this is a problem. A couple does not consist of three people.

Does she call everyday or several times a day? Does she call early in the morning? Even on weekends? Does she make up excuses to get him to come over and stay for hours? Does she try to sabotage your plans by making up some kind of emergency? Does she insist on being included in everything? These are key signs that you are in the middle of a power struggle. Don't give up hope. I have some tools you can use and please do so early in the marriage.

Establish Boundaries

Ask his mother to call on his cell phone so she doesn't disturb the whole family, especially if she likes to call early in the morning.

Don't discuss personal issues with either set of parents. Chances are you are going to make up and the matter is resolved. However, if you involve them, now they have a negative view of your spouse. Remember, a marriage does not consist of three people. <u>Learn to talk to each other – not about each other.</u> Don't allow parents to bad mouth your spouse. This is your choice and the marital unit is to be respected.

Suggest he goes by to see his mother one day each week. She can cook him a meal and they can catch up. If there are any repairs needed, he can do them while he's there. Meanwhile, you can go to the beauty shop or nail salon. A little pamper time goes a long way. Or if you prefer, you can spend time pursuing your interest or take a nap. Everybody needs some quiet time.

I often suggest that my husband go by a little more frequently and check on his mother, especially after the death of his father. I wanted him to know that I was concerned about her well being. A few years ago, we had a surprise birthday party for her at our home. Also, I've gone shopping with her because she doesn't have any daughters. When your man sees you are trying to work with his mother, you will be his center of attention.

Make Family Traditions

Cooking comes naturally to my mother-in law. Her favorite thing is cooking Thanksgiving dinner. However, my husband likes a big holiday meal at our home as well. Therefore, I have Thanksgiving Eve dinner with my husband and children. This way we can still celebrate at her home on Thanksgiving Day.

Make a big deal of her birthday and Mother's Day. Invite both his mom and your mom to a brunch on Mother's Day. Make sure you have a card and flowers. For her birthday, try to find out what she likes so the present can be meaningful. For example, if she likes perfume – find out what kind.

I'm sure you like to spend time with your side of the family. Establish when you both will visit each side together. You are a married couple now and should do things together. When the children come along, arrange for them to spend with both sets of grandparents. Grand children and grand parents should have a special bond.

Ten

You Got Him- Keep Him

OK, you married the love of your life and envision growing old together. I remember how excited I was when Dwayne and I were newlyweds. We called each other all day long and couldn't wait to get home in the evenings. We spent all of our time together thinking about and planning our future. I think the first few years of marriage should be spent focusing on each other. Many young women bring up the topic of when to start a family. I suggest waiting a couple of years after you are married.

Believe it or not, many marriages end in divorce within the first two years. The honeymoon is over and you get to see your husband in his natural state. If you didn't do your homework, you may not like what you see. That critical question comes up again. Ask yourself "Do I want to live the rest of my life this way?" If the answer is no, please don't bring a child into a marriage that is headed for disaster.

During our first year of marriage, Dwayne and I bought our first house. The second year, we took our dream vacation to Hawaii. During our third year, our daughter Danielle was born. Three years later, our son Dwayne II was born. They were born into a loving and happy home.

Over the years, I've noticed that the birth of a child can add stress to a marriage. Therefore, I've interviewed husbands to figure out why they leave home after they have a house full of children. The most common response is they feel like they have been replaced by the children. Their wives totally forget about them and only focus on the children.

They feel lonely and ignored. Armed with this knowledge, we must work harder to keep our men happy and involved.

How can you accomplish this? I have several suggestions and they all have worked for me. I am sure you've heard that old phrase "It takes a village to raise a child". I believe it does. There is no reason why other responsible adults can't help you with your children.

I made the decision to return to work three months after the birth of my children. Dwayne had the morning shift. He was responsible for dressing the children and dropping them off at the baby sitter's house. We were very fortunate to have both sets of grandparents and my wonderful sister-in-law Renee care for our children while we worked. He put on whatever outfits he liked. I never complained or criticized him even if they didn't match.

After work, I picked up the children and established bath and bedtime rituals. They were in bed by 8:30 p.m., so Dwayne and I could catch up on the events of the day. Ladies, do not try to be Super Mom. Ask for help and take it.

When your children are potty trained, develop a play group with your best friends and their children. It's a great way for them to make new friends and develop their social skills. You and your husband will have one night out each month. You can enjoy some time together by going to a romantic dinner and a show.

As the children grew, we were fortunate enough to take them on several family vacations. This is a great way for your husband to stay involved. Let him pick the vacation spots and interact with the children.

One thing most ladies don't learn is how to let your man be the head of the household. If you've done your homework, don't you trust him to take care of his family? Learn when to speak up and when to remain silent. This takes practice – trust me!

My husband and daughter have spent many afternoons together and they went on several "Daddy-Daughter Dates". He feels it's his job to show her how a lady is to be treated. When he hangs out with our son, they are doing some "male bonding". He takes a lot of time with him explaining things from the male perspective.

Remember ladies, you and your husband may have different strategies for reaching a goal. However, when the goal is reached, celebrate the accomplishment and remain his center of attention.

Eleven

Weekly Dates

Sooner or later your children will enter school full time. Also, they will develop interest in extracurricular activities. Do not overload your children or your husband. When my children were growing up, we allowed them to pick one activity at a time. They also had to stay on the honor roll in order to participate in any activities.

Over the years, my daughter was involved in ballet lessons, volleyball, basketball, track and field, choir and band. However, not at the same time. I always discussed scheduling with my husband so we could watch her performances and attend her games. We sat together and held hands.

My son was involved in tumbling, track and field, basketball, and the school band. We did the same with him and considered it a mini-date. Ladies, don't just pass by your husband in the morning while getting your kids off to school. Take time to be with him.

Do you remember how much time you spent getting ready for your dates before you got married? I'm sure your hair, nails and makeup had to be "just right". Do you still wear those cute outfits? If not, why not? Pull them out of your closet and put them to use. Get your sexy back!! Remember, men are visual human beings. I'm sure this is what attracted him to you in the first place.

Do you remember what it was like when it was just the two of you? What are some of the things you did together? Why not continue them? Just because you are married with children doesn't mean the fun has to stop.

We go on dates once a week. I usually let him pick the restaurants because I like all kinds of food. I always flirt with him and the children would hear me say that I'm going out with my boyfriend named Oscar. This is Dwayne's middle name. We go to a concert or play once a quarter.

Also, do small things for your husband regularly. Don't wait for a special occasion. My husband likes ice cream. I'll bring him his favorite flavor as a surprise in the middle of the week. I also collect memorabilia of his favorite recording artist for him. I love yellow flowers and chocolate. He'll bring some home and say, "I was just thinking of you."

We take two vacations each year - one with the children and one without. During the madness of raising our kids with hectic schedules, I still felt like I was the center of attention.

Twelve

Your Legacy

Our youngest child will leave for college next year. Dwayne and I will be empty nesters. We have been very fortunate to see our children reach all of their milestones thus far. They are truly our pride and joy. Our children have been our primary focus, but now it's time to shift the focus back to each other. We love to travel and plan to visit the Bahamas and Aruba next year.

Unfortunately, I've met people over the years that divorce as soon as the youngest child leaves home. They've put their own happiness aside for years and feel that they have fulfilled their obligations. I remember when one of my cousins graduated from college, his parents were divorced the following week.

I feel it's time to reiterate a few critical points. Success is achieved when preparation meets opportunity. You will have numerous opportunities to meet men anytime you leave your house. Are you prepared to do your homework?

Take your sweet time getting to know him. Look at your relationship carefully and objectively. It is – what it is. Is he abusive in any way, shape, or form? Do you detect any evidence of gambling, alcohol, or drug addiction? Don't make excuses for him and don't sign up for this.

Accept the fact <u>today</u> that you cannot change him. Remember, love doesn't hurt. Ask yourself that critical question. "Do I want to live the rest of my life this way?" If the answer is no, cut your losses and move on.

I recommend every woman live alone for at least two years. This will give you the self confidence you need to know you can make it on your own. I lived by myself for three years before I got married. I found my own apartment, signed my lease, and paid all of my own bills. This was a great learning experience and many women miss this if they move from their parent's home into an apartment with their boyfriend or husband.

If you find yourself in a bad relationship or marriage, you will have the confidence to leave and say to yourself, "I did it before and I can do it again. I do not want to live the rest of my life this way." Remember, you are whole with or without a man.

If you make the decision to enter into a marriage, be prepared to work with your husband to build a life together. Work is an action word. Marriage takes a great deal of work, but look at the possibilities of what you can create with the one you love.

Will your children have fond memories of their childhood and take their time looking for love? Or will they leave home as soon as possible – even if they move in with a man who is abusive or addicted to gambling, drugs, or alcohol? If this is the environment you have created, don't be surprised because this is all they know. Changing your own lives will change the future of your children. What will your legacy be?

My husband is teaching me how to play golf and we still laugh together. Even after all of these years, I still catch him staring at me from across the room. We hold hands all the time. His favorite color is red. Needless to say, I have numerous outfits in all shades of red.

He recently gave me a card for Mother's Day that said, "If I had to do it all over again, I know that I'd choose you." We are planning our 25th wedding anniversary celebration. If we can do it, so can you. You can live happily ever after while remaining his center of attention throughout your whole marriage.

Afterword

As you continue your journey through life, use these tools to guide you. They are timeless and I truly hope you share them with your daughter someday. If you know a woman in need, please share them with her as well.

You may encounter some difficulties, but now you have the self confidence to pull through and change your situation accordingly. Remember my motto - Success is achieved when preparation meets opportunity!

Keep your standards high as you look for your prince. This way you will always remain his center of attention.

Made in the USA
Middletown, DE
08 February 2020

84261807R00040